FROM THE LIBRARY OF

BEAR RIGHT

AN UNEXBEARGATED
COMPBEARHENSIVE
INCOMPBEARABLE

BOOK OF

CELEBEARTIES
& OTHER BEARS

BY PHYLLIS DEMONG

J. M. DENT & SONS LTD
London Toronto Melbourne

First published in Great Britain 1980

Copyright © 1979 by Phyllis Demong

Printed in Great Britain by
Biddles Ltd, Guildford for
J. M. Dent & Sons Ltd
Aldine House, Welbeck Street, London

British Library Cataloguing in Publication Data

Demong, Phyllis
    Celebearties & other bears.
    1. American wit and humor, Pictorial
    2. Bears—Caricatures and cartoons
    I. Title
    741.5'973   NC1429

    ISBN 0–460–04506 7

FOR
DEE
HEYWOOD

INTRODUCTION

FROM BEARKLEY CAL-
IFORNIA TO THE BEAR-
RING SEA, FROM BEARNE
SWITZERLAND TO
NORTHERN SIBEARIA,
THE WORLD HAS LONG
YEARNED AND BEARNED
FOR A COMPBEARHEN-
SIVE INCOMPBEARABLE
UNEXBEARGATED BOOK
OF BEARS
AND HERE IT IS . . .

THIS BOOK HAS BEEN
BRUIN FOR QUITE A-
WHILE, AND THOUGH
FILLED WITH PUNS
BOTH BEARABLE AND
UNBEARABLE, IT
REPBEARSENTS ONLY THE
TIP OF THE ICEBEARG.
  ACKNOWLEDGEMENT
IS DUE TO THOSE WHO
HELPED BEAR THE
BEARDEN OF SCHOLARLY
RESEARCH • TO TIM
ATKINS OF THE BEAR
NECESSITIES (THE
BEARON OF THE BEAR IN-
DUSTRY • WITH SHOPS
COAST-TO-COAST) TO HIS
ASSISTANT BARBEARA—
TO JEAN BEARADSHAW
LYTTLE—AND TO MY DOG
BEARANDY WHOSE BEAR-
LIKE NOSE HAS BEEN A
CONSTANT INSBEARATION
• BEARCI • (THAT'S
FRENCH FOR THANK
YOU). THE AUTHOR

MIDDLEBEARY, BEARMONT

CELEBEARTIES

RICHARD BEARTON

SARAH BEARNHART

the Divine Beara

LIBEARACE
(holding candleabeara)

VICTOR HERBEART
(writing an opbearetta)

JOHN BEARRYMORE
(as Shakesbeare's Hamlet)

HERBEART HOOBEAR

A BEARHAM LINCOLN

SCHUBEART

LEONARD BEARNSTEIN

(conducting Bearlioz)

THEDA BEARA

HANK GREENBEARG

YOGI BEARRA

BEARNARD BEARUCH

FATHER BEARIGAN

BEAR   BRYANT

MAX BEAR

BRIDGET BEARDOT

ALBEART EINSTEIN

BEARYSHNIKOV

SAINTE BEARNADETTE

IZABETH BEARETT BROWNING

JAMES BEARD

B'EAR RABBIT

BEART LAHR
(as the Cowardly Lion)

THE BEAR
THAT MADE
MILWAUKEE
FAMOUS

MISS ABEARICA

BEART PARKS

BEARON ROTHSCHILD
bearing beargundy wine

GEORGE BEARNARD SHAW

MORE CELEBEARTIES

NNA BEARIA ALBEARGHETTI
ANDY BEARGEN
IGLEBEAR HUMPBEARDINK
EARGESS MEREDITH
LBEART CAMUS
EARBARA STANWYCK
LLAN GINSBEARG
UBEART HUMBEARY
OUIS KRONENBEARGER
EN BEARNIE
TRINDBEARG
T. BEARNUM
LGERNON SWINBEARNE
AMES THURBEAR
YRANO DE BEARGERAC
MBROSE BEARCE
HORNTON BEARGESS
ICHARD CHAMBEARLIN
UBE GOLDBEARG
OHN BEARCH (SOCIETY)
RIZZLY ADAMS
EARPEE (SEEDS)
ENERAL BEARGOYNE
ARON BEARR
INCE LOMBEARDI
ALLACE BEARY
UBREY BEARDSLEY

CAROL BEARNETT
DAVID BEARINKLEY
BEARY MANILOW
KATHERINE HEPBEARN
GINA LOLLABEARIDGIDA
DR. CHRISTIAN BEARNARD
BLUEBEARD
ROBEART REDFORD
BEARTOLUCCI
BEART LANCE
CLAUDETTE COLBEAR
INGRID BEARGMAN
INGMAR BEARGMANN
BEARY GOLDWATER
ELY CULBEARTSON
BEARTHOLD BRECHT
ANN MORROW LINDBEARGH
RALPH WALDO EMBEARSON
ROBEART E. LEE
WILBEAR WRIGHT
BARBEARA STREISAND
GUSTAVE FLAUBEART
ROBEART FROST
CARL SANDBEARG
BARBEARA WALTERS
BEAR ABBIE
JOHN BEARSFORD TIPTON

& MORE!

CHE GUEBEARRA
DIANE VON FURSTENBEARG
FREDDIE BEARTHOLOMEW
EPHRIAM ZIMBEARLIST
KING HUMBEARTO
FABEARGE
SHELLEY BEARMAN
BEARLITZ
ELLEN BEARSTYN
BEARIO ANDRETTI
WOODWARD & BEARNSTEIN
SIR JAMES BEARRIE

BELA BEARTOK
SIR MAX BEARBOHM
BEARENDAN BEHAN
HUCKLEBEARY FINN
MARISA BEARENSEN
MILTON BEARLE
IRVING BEARLIN
HEYWOOD BRUIN
JOHN BEARLYCORN
BEARTHSHEBA
SAMUEL BEARBER

BEAR LINES

_____
_____
_____
_____
_____
_____
_____

_____
_____
_____
_____
_____
_____
_____

FAMILY,
OCCUPATIONS
& ACTIVITIES

BIRTH ANNOUNCEMENT

A NEW CUB!
Bearyl Bearginia

FORE

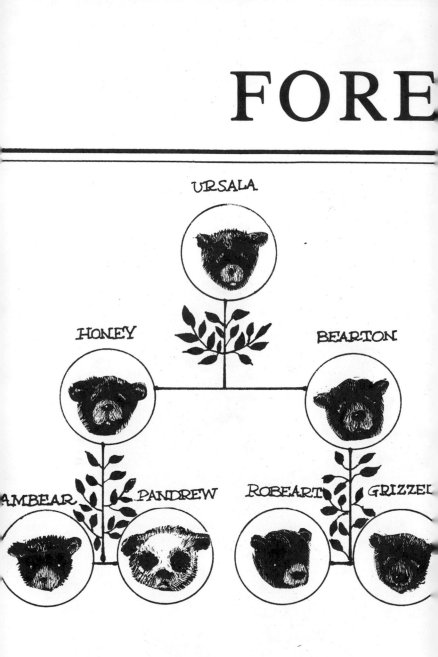

URSALA

HONEY

BEARTON

AMBEAR

PANDREW

ROBEART

GRIZZEL

BEARS

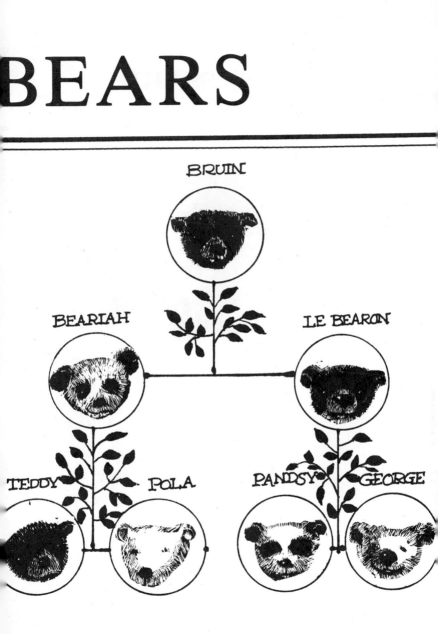

BRUIN

BEARIAH   LE BEARON

TEDDY   POLA   PANDSY   GEORGE

AUNT BEARTHA
WITH BEARNIECE

THE BEARRIES

LINGONBEARY • TEABEARY
STRAWBEARY • BLUEBEARY
HUCKLEBEARY • GOOSEBEARY
RAZZBEARY • BOYSENBEARY

&THE ELDERBEARRY

BEAR CHEST

EMBEARASSED

LUMBEARJACK
with bearch tree

TIM BEAR

BEAR HUG

BEARRELING DOWNHILL
(bearallel skier)

OPBEARATOR.......

WOMEN'S LIBBEAR
bearning her bearssiere

BEARING GIFTS   BEARING AR

.......**BEARING CHILDREN**

SOMBEARO

HABEARDASHER

BEARET

APBEARATIF

SOBEAR

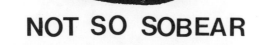

NOT SO SOBEAR

"BEARP"

BARBEARSHOP QUARTET

UMBEARELLA

BARRISTER

bear aspbearin

 **AND**

BEARTENDER
INEBEARATED
BEARSERK
BEAROMETER
BEARRICADE
BEARBACK RIDER
BEARI-BEARI
SCARLET FEBEAR
AMBEARGRIS

NEIGHBEARS
BEAR-ENTHESES
ROBBEARS
SLOBBEARS
TROOPBEARS
(SMOKIES)
BEAREAVED
BEAR SKIN RUG

AND
SOME LEFTOBEARS FOR BEARUNC

BEARMUDA ONIONS
HAMBEARGERS
BEARNAISE SAUCE
ASBEARAGAS
ICEBEARG LETTUCE
CUCUMBEARS
BEARGAMOT TEA
HUBBEARD SQUASH
CAMEMBEART
BEARRIES
BEARLEY SOUP

BEAROWNIES
RHUBEARB
POPOBEARS
CORN BEARED
BEAR-B-QUE
BEARANDY
   ALEXANDER
PUMPBEARNIKEL
LOX AND BEARGEL
BEARST OF CHICK.
BEARETZELS

ASSOCIATES

DAMONIUM!

PANDALOONS

SUSPANDARS

EXPAN

DABLE

NURSA
(with hypbearderm

URSA MAJOR
URSA MINOR

POLA

EAR ON ICEBEARG

POLAR

POLA

COCA KOALA
PEPSI KOALA

EKOALATY

NIGHT KOALA

KOALING ON HANDS & KNEES

AND.......
OBSCENE PHONE KOALA

TEDDY ROOSEVELT

A TEDDY

AND

PANDAMERICA
PANDAORA'S BOX
PANDAHELLENIC
URSATZ
PURSANALITY
STEDDY
UNSTEDDY
TEDDY PHONE
TEDDY GRAPH
TEDDY VISION
NUMBEARS (POLAR BEARS)

RELATED SUBJECTS

BEARITONE
(singing 'If ebear I would leave ye

BEAR BEARREL POLKA

♭🎼 CIRI ♪ BEARI ♪ BIN ♪

O beary me not on the lone prairie

bears eat oats
'n does eat oats'n

♪♪"eating goobear peas"♪♪

wh' oan cha be ma teddy bear

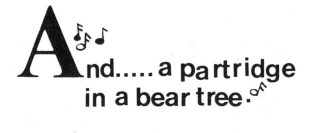

And..... a partridge in a bear tree.

follies beargère

BEAROQUE MUSIC
ABEARICA THE BEAUTIFUL
THE NIGHTINGALE SANG IN
  BEARKLEY SQUARE
BEAR WENT OVER THE MOUNTAIN
I FOUND MY LOVE ON BLUE-
  BEARRY HILL
THE YELLOW SUBEARINE

BEAR
THESE DATES IN MIND

HAPPY BEARTHDAYS

BEAR MITZVAHS

ANNIBEARSARIES

SEPTEMBEAR

LABEAR DAY

BACK TO BEAROWN UNIBEARS

OCTOBEAR

NOVEMBEAR

DECEMBEAR

BEARRE   BEARMONT
BEARLINGTON BEARMONT
GREAT BEARRINGTON MASS.
BEARMINGHAM ALABEARMA
BEAR MT. N.Y.
BEARGEN NORWAY
BEARNE SWITZERLAND
PITTSBEARGH PA.
HARRIS-BEARGH PA.
WILKES BEARRE PA.
BEARKLEY CA.
BEARLIN GER.
BEARGUNDY FR.
BEARMUDA
BEARIA KY.
KOALA LAMPUR, MALA.
N. BRUINSWICK CANADA
S. BEARWICK ME.
BEARMA
BEARBANK CA.
IBEARIA
SIBEARIA USSR
GIBEARALTER
ALBEARTA CANADA

GS STRAIT

LIBEARIA AFRICA
JOHANNESBEARG S.A.
BEARCELONA SPAIN
BEARU S.A.
BEARMA
EDINBEARGH SCOT.
ABEARDEEN SCOT.
BEARUT

ATLAS

OLD SAYINGS · PROBEARBS

BEAR AND FOREBEAR
  IS GOOD PHILOSOP

KOALA ME ANYTHING
  BUT DON'T KOALA
  LATE FOR DINNER

LIBEARTY EKOALATY
  AND FRATERNITY

REMEMBEAR THE MA

BEAR WITH ME

GRIN AND BEAR IT

A LABEAR OF LOVE

GOD BLESS ABEARICA

BEARIN GO BRAGH

MOTTOS · QUOTES · CLICHÉS ·

ARKING UP THE WRONG TREE

E KOALATY OF MERCY IS NOT STRAINED . . . .

H BIN EIN BEARLINER"

/INO BEARITAS

AR FOOT BOY WITH CHEEK OF TAN . . . .

T ON YOUR BEARAKES

AR RIGHT—BEAR LEFT

RIVABEARCI ROMA

SELL A BEAR ! TO SELL WHAT ONE HAS NOT

FIDDLE WHILE ROME BEARNS

OM BEARAKE OF DAY 'TIL SETTING SUN
WOMAN'S WORK IS NEBEAR DONE

BEAR PAGE

"LOVE BEARS ALL THINGS, BELIEVES
ALL THINGS, ENDURES ALL THINGS."

I CORINTHIANS 13-4

BEAR LEFT